TRINITY'S GIRL 90 DAY DEVOTIONAL

A 90 Day devotional inspired by the Holy Spirit to encourage women of all Spiritual levels to develop a deeper personal relationship with the Trinity.

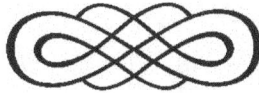

CATHERINE STERLING

Trinity's Girl 90 Day Devotional,

by Catherine Sterling ISBN # 978-1-64660-002-1

Copyright © 2019 By Catherine Sterling

Published by

Trinity's Girl Ministries

All Scripture references are taken from the New King James Version

To:

FROM:

Acknowledgements

I thank the Father, the Son and the Holy Spirit who planted, nurtured, pruned, and most of all, loves me unconditionally.

A special thanks to my daughter Tori Sterling, who always believes in me and works hard to help me along my every journey.

To all of Trinity's Girls who have a desire for a more intimate walk with the Lord.

Much Love to the ladies whom God planted for me to minister to and those He appointed to be my mothers, sisters, friends, prayer warriors, mentors, and motivators, may God continue to bless you all!

Introduction

This devotional is anointed to heal, deliver, and set the captive free! Trinity's Girl devotional is 90 days of powerful scriptures and personal experiences with the Trinity! The contents of this book will encourage the reader to develop a deeper personal relationship with the Father, Son, and the Holy Spirit. Using scriptures directly from the Bible to build a bridge into the presence of the Trinity; a deeper, renewed, and restored walk with our Lord.

Divided into thirteen inspirations, it has one inspired topic a week for ninety days, a prayer for each week and truths to remember.

There is also scripture references and declarations, one for each day of the week.

Day seven is a final day to reflect on what the Trinity is speaking to the reader. Prepare for 90 days of restoration.

Table of Contents

WEEK 1

SEEK THE LORD WHOLEHEARTEDLY

The Scripture

Hebrews 11:6 "But without faith, it is impossible to please Him, for he who comes to God must believe that He is, and that He is a rewarder of those who diligently seek Him."

The Experience

Hebrews 11:6 came to life for me during a conversation with my daughter; she was excited about having ministered the word of God to one of my sons, her oldest brother. She proclaimed to him the importance of faith how we must have it. She quoted, "Now faith is substance of things hoped for and the evidence of things not seen," I reminded her where to find this scripture. She grabbed her Bible and flipped the pages to Hebrew chapter 11 as she read, we both began to cry; I was so excited to hear my child calling the word of God beautiful! As we read verse 6, the words diligently seek, and rewarder jumped off the page at me, and I knew God was inviting me to seek Him wholeheartedly.

The Word

Throughout the Bible, the Lord continues to invite us to seek Him; therefore, we should seek the Lord before we seek our daily needs because He is faithful to provide. The Lord promises in **Proverbs 8:17** "I love those who love me, and those who seek me diligently will find me." The Lord is not inviting us to seek what He can do for us wholeheartedly, but He wants us to seek Him wholeheartedly. We should study to have a closer personal relationship with the father. The Lord 's ways are higher than our ways, He knows all things, and when we are in a relationship with Him, then we know that we can see Him in every situation of our lives. We can seek Him for repentance, direction, and guidance. We should continually seek to know the Lord.

Daily Prayer: My Lord and my savior Jesus Christ, my friend, my everything, as always, I need you. I need your presence, and Lord touch my mind as I read these words and give me a desire to diligently seek you. Lord, may I be mindful that you are my rewarder, mindful of how much you want me to draw near unto you and how much you love me. Thank you, Lord for looking out for my family and friends, and giving them desires to know you more. Thank you, Jesus!

DAILY SCRIPTURES FOR MEDITATING

Day 1

Isaiah 55:6. "Seek the Lord while he may be found, call upon him while he is near,"

Declare Today

I will seek the Lord with urgency!

Remember

Seek to know him more intimately!

Day 2

Hebrew 11:6 "but without faith it is impossible to please Him, for he who comes to God must believe that He is, and that He is a rewarder of those who diligently seek Him."

Declare Today

I will seek God by faith!

Remember

Seek him continuously.

Day 3

Proverbs 8:17 "I love those who love me, and those who seek me diligently will find me."

Declare Today

I shall find God when I seek Him diligently!

Remember

Seek Him for a closer relationship.

Day 4

Matthew 6:33 "but seek ye first the kingdom of God and his righteousness and all these things shall be added unto you."

Declare Today

If I seek God first, He will provide all my needs!

Remember

Seek Him for direction!

Day 5

2nd Chronicles 7:14 "If my people who are called by my name will humble themselves and pray and seek my face and turn from their wicked ways then will I hear from heaven forgive their sin and heal their land"

Declare Today

I will humble myself, pray, and seek God in times of repentance!

Remember

Seek Him in spirit and in truth!

Day 6

Colossians 3:1 "if then you were raised with Christ, seek those things which are above, where Christ is sitting at the right hand of God. Set your mind on things above not on things on the earth"

Declare Today

I will purposely keep my mind on Christ!

Remember

Seek Him in our worship, praise, and our prayers.

Day 7

Are you seeking God whole heartily? What is the Trinity saying to you? What was your takeaway from this week's topic? /Notes.

_____
_____
_____
_____
_____
_____
_____
_____
_____
_____
_____
_____
_____
_____
_____
_____
_____
_____
_____
_____
_____
_____
_____
_____
_____
_____

WEEK 2

GOD'S FAITHFULNESS TO HIS DISCIPLES

(DORCAS THE DISCIPLE)

The Scripture

Acts 9:36-40 "At Joppa, there was a certain disciple named Tabitha, which is translated as Dorcas. This woman was full of good works and charitable deeds which she did. But it happened in those days that she became sick and died. When they had washed her, they laid her in an upper room. And since Lydda was near Joppa, and the disciples had heard that Peter was there, they sent two men to him, imploring him not to delay in coming to them. Then Peter arose and went with them. When he had come, they brought him to the upper room. And all the widows stood by him weeping, showing the tunics and garments which Dorcas had made while she was with them. But Peter put them all out and knelt down and prayed. And turning to the body, he said, "Tabitha, arise." And she opened her eyes, and when she saw Peter, she sat up."

The Experience

I was once invited to be a speaker at a women's conference at my church. The theme was the women of the Bible, and I was assigned Dorcas also known as Tabatha. This was a big thing for me because it was my first time speaking to anyone other than my church family. I had lots of time to prepare, so I asked the Holy Spirit what I should do, and He suggested that I see Dorcas relationship with the Father, Son, and the Holy Spirit. I studied Dorcas, and I found myself in her.

The Bible didn't tell the story of Dorcas before she knew Jesus, I can only imagine that she was an orphan, a drinker of much wine, a struggling single mom, maybe like you or me. We do know her as disciplined in the things of Christ, so I can imagine that she found Jesus and He took her in His arms, interceded to the father for her and introduced her to the Holy Spirit; that's what he did for me. Dorcas did good works; she made the father's business her main priority. Her relationship with the Trinity multiplied her gift, she was Swift about the things of God, and she gave out of her nothing! Dorcas obedience and her love for the people earned her a meeting in the upper room when it looked like it was over. God sent Peter filled with the Holy Spirit to call her name, and when called upon once again, she answered the call and arose to serve another day.

The Word

The Bible refers to Dorcas as a disciple, a woman full of good works, and charitable deeds which she did. This suggests that she was not only filled with good works, but she also did them. However, it happened in those days that she became sick and died. When they had washed her and laid her in the upper room, God strategically placed Peter at Joppa filled with the Holy Spirit just for Tabitha (Dorcas). We were given the testimonies of disciples, like Dorcas throughout the scriptures as an example; Tabitha's testimony was a true witness to God's Faithfulness. The Bible says in **Acts 9:42** "And it became known throughout all Joppa and many believe on the Lord" When we stand up for Him, He will stand for us and no matter the situation, He will raise us up. He rewards us when we feed His sheep, when we care for others from our hearts.

Daily prayer: Lord, thank you for giving me an opportunity to serve you, an opportunity to use the gifts and talents that you have given me for your glory!! Lord teach me to be a disciple like Dorcas, to give my talents and resources for the good of others. In Jesus name I pray, Amen!

DAILY SCRIPTURE FOR MEDITATION

Day 1

Acts 9:37 "But it happened in those days that she became sick and died. When they had washed her, they laid her in an upper room."

Declare Today

Jesus will meet me in my time of trouble!

Remember

Trust God to meet you in your place of need.

Day 2

Acts 9:38 "And since Lydia was near Joppa, and the disciples had heard that Peter was there, they sent two men to him, imploring him not to delay in coming to them."

Declare Today

In my time of need, God will send the right people at the right time!

Remember

God has already prepared the answer you need!

Day 3

Acts 9:39 "then Peter arose and went with them when he had come, they brought him to the upper room and all the widows stood by him weeping showing the tunics and garments which Dorcas had made while she was with them."

Declare Today

I will be of service to those around me!

Remember

A relationship with the trinity will give us access to the upper room.

Day 4

Acts 9:40 "But Peter put them all out and knelt down and prayed. And turning to the body he said, Tabatha arise. And she opened her eyes, and when she saw Peter she sat up."

Declare Today

Like Peter, I will remove all distractions when I pray!

Remember

God can and will raise you up from your dark place.

Day 5

Acts 9:41 "Then he gave her his hand and lifted her up; and when he had called the Saints and widows, he presented her alive."

Declare Today

I will extend a hand to lift someone up!

Remember

Present life to those around you.

Day 6

Acts 9:42 "And it became known throughout all Joppa and many believe on the Lord"

Declare Today

I will testify of the works of the Lord everywhere I go!

Remember

These signs will follow those who believe.

Day 7

Do you know the meaning of the word disciple? What is the Trinity saying to you? What was your takeaway from this week's   topic?   Notes.

WEEK 3

GIVE TO THE LORD

Scripture

1 **Chronicles 16:28-29** "Give to the Lord all families of the people, give to the Lord glory and strength. Give to the Lord the glory due his name bring an offering and come before him oh, worship the Lord in the beauty of his holiness."

The Experience

God notices when we are not thankful. Remember ten healed lepers, only one returned to say thank you, Jesus noticed! I learned that if we dare to give God thanks in all things, that if we adore and worship him with our whole heart, it strengthens our relationship. Our association with

Him is what makes us holy, and holiness is determined by the quality of your holy. Give yourself to God. The closer you are to God, the more you can walk in holiness. Holiness is where we need to be (in His presence)! Give of yourself to the Lord; He's mighty in power, and He cares for you. Lose all fear!

The word

The writer was encouraging the people to give Glory to God, to thank Him, adore, and worship Him, for all He had done. Come into his presence with offerings and enjoy the beauty of His presence, the beauty of who He is and worship Him there.

We can't beat God giving, He already gave it all, when you give to God you Win! John 3:16 "For God so loved the world that he gave his only begotten Son, that whoever believes in him should not perish but have everlasting life." We can't beat that!! God will multiply our gifts, talents, and time.

Daily Prayer: Lord Father God, creator of heaven and earth, thank you, thank you, thank you! All my praise goes to you! I honor and adore you! Lord thank you for giving me an attitude of gratitude, renewing a thankful heart within me. Lord, thank you that my first response will be thanksgivings, honor, and adoration, Lord, thank you that your mercy endures forever! Thank you, Jesus!

DAILY SCRIPTURE FOR MEDITATING

Day 1

1 Chronicles 16:28-29 "28: Give to the Lord all families of the people, give to the Lord glory and strength. 29: Give to the Lord the glory due his name bring an offering and come before him oh, worship the Lord in the beauty of holiness!"

Declare Today

I will give to the Lord glory due to His name.

Remember

Give an offering unto the Lord.

Day 2

Psalm 24:1 "The earth is the Lords and all its fullness, the world and those who dwell therein."

Declare Today

The earth and everything in it belong to the Lord.

Remember

Give God thanks in all things.

Day 3

Psalm 66:8-9 "Oh, bless our God, you people! And make the voice of his praise to be heard, who keeps our soul among the living, and does not allow our feet to be moved."

Declare Today

I will praise the Lord with a loud voice.

Remember

Give God continuous praise!

Day 4

Acts 3:6 "Then Peter said, silver and gold I do not have, but what I do have I give you: In the name of Jesus Christ of Nazareth rise up and walk."

Declare Today

I will give unto others what I do have.

Remember

Give your time unto the Lord!

Day 5

Luke 17:17-19 So Jesus answered and said, "Were there not 10 cleanest? But where are the nine?" Were there not any found who returned to give glory to God except his foreigner?" And he said to him arise go your way your faith has made you well."

Declare Today

I will always give thanks to God!

Remember

Give God thanks!

Day 6

1 Chronicles 16:34 "Oh Give thanks to the Lord, for he is good! For his mercy endures forever!"

Declare Today

Gods Mercy towards me endures forever.

Remember

Give yourself unto the Lord!

Day 7

What are you willing to give unto the Lord? What is God saying to you? / What was your takeaway from this week's topic? /Notes.

_____

_____

_____

_____

_____

_____

_____

_____

_____

_____

_____

_____

_____

_____

_____

_____

_____

_____

_____

_____

_____

_____

WEEK 4

PURPOSE TO KNOW THE VOICE OF GOD

The Scripture

1 John 4:1-4 "Beloved, do not believe every spirit, but test the spirits, whether they are of God; because many false prophets have gone out into the world. By this you know the Spirit of God: Every spirit that confesses that Jesus Christ has come in the flesh is of God, and every spirit that does not confess that Jesus Christ has come in the flesh is not of God. And this is the spirit of the Antichrist, which you have heard was coming, and is now already in the world. You are of God, little children, and have overcome them because He who is in you is greater than he who is in the world."

The Experience

There are so many voices and many distractions in the world. I have learned that I must purposely seek to know and hear the voice of God and this requires relationship with the trinity. I have also found that the Father, Son, and Holy Spirit are the best teachers, and that when I purposely lean in, ask, and be open to receive (study the scriptures) than I am able to discern truth, and through the power of the Spirit I am able to walk in truth!

God has given us the ability to hear His voice through the gift of Jesus, the scriptures and the Holy Spirit. It is now our duty to believe the word (for those who come to Him must believe that He is and that He is a rewarder of those who diligently seek him,). We must be doers of the word and not hearers only, and in doing, we imitate Jesus because He teaches us to hear the Father. When I allow God to be a part of my decision making on a daily basis, then I can be confident that no matter the outcome, no matter what; I can trust God! God is so good! Look for Jesus in your situation and do what He would do, listen to Jesus!

The Word

Jesus said that my sheep hear my voice and I know them, and they follow me, Jesus declares His love for His sheep. He says, "I'm the good shepherd and the good shepherd gives his life for the sheep," The shepherd walked so close to His sheep that they knew him, and He knew them. Jesus proclaims in **John 10:14** "I am the good shepherd and I know my sheep and I am known by my own." We are also invited to walk close to Jesus, He says that we are his! Hear his voice today, learn to hear him, lean in!

I will never leave you nor forsake you is what I hear the Spirit say in this moment!

Daily Prayer: Heavenly Father, creator of the world the Alpha and Omega, He who was, is and is to come. Lord, you chose me before the beginning of time you framed me, and you know me. Thank you, God that I am your sheep, and you are my shepherd, that you invite me to hear your voice and to draw near to you! Lord, thank you for your protection and care! In Jesus name I Pray! Amen!

DAILY SCRIPTURES FOR MEDITATING

Day 1

John 10:14 "I am the good shepherd and I know my sheep and I am known by my own."

Declare Today

To know Jesus is to be in relationship with Him!

Remember

Know the word for yourself!

Day 2

Romans 13:14 "But put on the Lord Jesus Christ and make no provision for the flesh to fulfil its lust."

Declare Today

If I abide in Jesus Christ, then there is no room for the lust of the flesh!

Remember

Know the truth and walk in it.

Day 3

John 10:16 "And other sheep I have which are not of this fold; them also I must bring, and they will hear my Voice and there will be one flock and one shepherd."

Declare Today

I will invite others to know the Lord's voice!

Remember

Know how to discern His voice.

Day 4

Psalm 95:7 "For he is our God, and we are the people of his pasture and the sheep of his hand."

Declare Today

God is our God, and we are His people!

Remember

Know who you are in Christ!

Day 5

John 18:37 Pilate, therefore, said to Him, "are you a King then?" Jesus answered, "You say rightly that I am a king. For this cause I was born, and for this cause I have come into the world, that I should bear witness to the truth. Everyone who is of the truth hears my voice."

Declare Today

Jesus is the truth, and everyone who accepts the truth hears His voice!

Remember

Know that you can hear the voice of God.

Day 6

Revelation 3:20 "Behold I stand at the door and knock, if anyone hears my voice and opens the door, I will come into him and dine with him, and he with me."

Declare Today

I will open the door to my heart for Jesus to come in.

Remember

Know the voice of the Spirit.

Day 7

What steps can you take to help you discern the voice of God? What is God saying to you? What was your takeaway from this week's topic? Notes.

WEEK 5

YOUR GIFT IS NEEDED IN THE KINGDOM OF GOD

The Scripture

Romans 12:6 "Having then gifts differing according to the grace that is given to us, let us use them: if prophecy, let us prophesy according to our faith; or ministry, Let us use it in our ministering; he who teaches, in teaching; he who exhorts, in exhortation; he who gives, with liberality; he who leads, with diligence; and he who shows mercy, with cheerfulness."

The Kingdom of God is the Kingdom of heaven, a real government established and ruled by God, and ruled from heaven. Jesus is our King and we are Kingdom citizens.

The Experience

God's Best gift to us is Jesus Christ (Hallelujah thank God for Jesus). As individuals, God has placed gifts, talents, and abilities on the inside of each of us, unique to us, He gave us all a measure, what we do with the measure given to us is our choice. It amazes me that everyone can see our gift but us. I believe your gift is that one thing that you can do better than others; it even bugs you when this area is being neglected by others. Ask God, what he wants you to do?

We all know that one beautician who has great talent but no desire to use it! Let's not be like that Beautician, when it concerns God's Kingdom. You can't delegate motherhood (in the Spirit), and don't try and pass your baby along to someone else. We have different destinies and destinations; do what God has called you to do, kicking and screaming, whatever it takes just do it! God needs your Gift (spiritual, physical, or atmosphere shifting gift) operating in the Kingdom at full potential! Do not despise your gift or small beginnings; and don't compare yourself to others, submit your gift to God! I Love God, He always takes my little and multiplies it! Use your gift to the glory of God and walk in His holiness from faith to faith. You may say, but I don't know what my gift is; I say commit to hearing the voice of God, be a willing vessel and the Trinity will empower your gift!

The Word

This week's scripture (Romans 12:6) describes the essence of our gifts; somewhere in our gift, one or all of these attributes are in operation. The word says according to the grace given to us, use them (our gifts), use our God given gifts! We are all gifted to be apart in fulfilling the great commission. We are disciples! **1 Timothy 4:13-15** "Do not neglect the gift that is in you, which was given to you by the prophecy with the laying on of hands of the eldership. Meditate on these things give yourself entirely to them that your progress may be evident to all."

All gifts are given from God, and He is no respecter of person. For by grace you have been saved through faith a gift from God, the giver of all gifts.

Daily Prayer: My heavenly Holy Father, my Lord and Savior Jesus Christ, Lord, I come to you as humble as I know how. Lord, I petition you on behalf of those reading these words, Lord thank you for the gift you have placed within me, thank you for giving me a desire to serve your people with those gifts, thank you for teaching me to be your hands and feet on earth, in Jesus name I pray Amen!

DAILY SCRIPTURES FOR MEDITATING

Day 1

1 Timothy 4:13-15 "Do not neglect the gift that is in you, which was given to you by the prophecy with the laying on of hands of the eldership. Meditate on these things give yourself entirely to them that your progress may be evident to all."

Declare Today

I will give myself, to the gift which is within me.

Remember

My gift is in God's will.

Day 2

Ephesians 2:8 "For by grace you have been saved through faith, and that not of yourselves; it is the gift of God."

Declare Today

God has given me the gift of salvation.

Remember

My God has a gift just for me.

Day 3

2 Timothy 1:6 "Therefore I remind you to stir up the gift of God which is in you through the laying on of my hands."

Declare Today

I will stir up the gift of God within me.

Remember

My Gift will make room for me.

Day 4

James 1:17 "every good and perfect gift is from above, and comes down from the Father of lights, with whom there is no variation or shadow of turning".

Declare Today

My gift is a perfect gift from God.

Remember

My God is the giver of all gifts.

Day 5

Romans 11:29 "For the gifts and the callings of God are irrevocable."

Declare Today

My gifts are from God and cannot be taken away.

Remember

My God's gifts are irrevocable.

Day 6

1 Corinthians 12:6 "And there are diversities of activities, but it is the same God who works all in all."

Declare Today

God is the giver of all gifts.

Remember

My God will reveal my Gift!

Day 7

What is your Kingdom gift? What is God saying to you? What was your takeaway from this week's topic? Notes.

WEEK 6

CHOOSE LIFE.

The Scripture

Matthew 7:13-14 "Enter in by the narrow gate: for wide is the gate and broad is the way that leads to destruction, and there are many who go in by it. Because narrow is the gate and difficult is the way which leads to life, and there are few who find it."

The Experience

I love Jesus because He loved me first, He chooses me, and He chose you! Reverence Him, acknowledge Him, love him, obey Him, take Him at his word, and trust Him. Beloved, we have got to be all in when it comes to our relationship with Jesus. He wants us to have all that the Father promised, Jesus knows the hardships and battles we fight, so He never leaves us. He picks us up every time we fall, and He directs us! In all the noise of this busy world, have an ear to hear Jesus say take the narrow gate;

The Word

Jesus is giving us firm instructions on which gate to choose. He says choose the narrow gate which leads to life, and this life Jesus speaks of is eternal. Jesus points out that only few will find it, the narrow gate which leads to life. Jesus is saying the road may be tough, but we must stay the narrow course.

Matthew 7:13 "Wide is the gate, and broad is the way that leads to destruction" There is destruction all around us, but as long we abide in Jesus Christ, it shall not come near us.

Daily Prayer: My father, my Lord and Savior Jesus Christ, Lord, I come before you as humble as I know how, arms uplifted, thanking you! Thank you for choosing me, thank you Lord for leading me to the narrow gate, and thank you, Lord for protecting me and looking out for me along the way! Nothing can separate me from your love. Thank you, Jesus amen!

DAILY SCRIPTURES FOR MEDITATING

Day 1

Matthew 13:24 "Strive to enter through the narrow gate, for many I say to you, will seek to enter and will not be able."

Declare Today

I seek to enter the narrow gate on purpose.

Remember

Stay close to Jesus.

Day 2

Duet 30:15-16 "See, I have set before you today life and good, death and evil, and that I command you today to love the Lord your God to walk in his ways and to keep his commandments, His statues, His judgments, that you may live and multiply; and the Lord your God will bless you in the land which you go to possess."

Declare Today

I choose life and good, I love the Lord God, and I choose to walk in His ways and follow His commandments.

Remember

Stay in faith!

Day 3

Deuteronomy 30:19 "I called heaven and earth as witnesses today against you, that I have set before you life and death, blessing and cursing; therefore choose life, that both you and your descendants may live;"

Declare Today

Life and death are set before me, but on behalf of my descendants I choose life.

Remember

Stay the course.

Day 4

1 King 18:21 "And Elijah came to all the people, and said, how long will you falter between two opinions? If the Lord is God, follow him; but if Baal, follow him, but the people answered him not a word."

Declare Today

The Lord is God, and I will follow Him.

Remember

Stay on the Lord's side!

Day 5

John 6:66 "From that time many of his disciples went back and walked with him no more."

Declare Today

I will forever walk with Jesus! Jesus is the way!

Remember

Stay focused!

Day 6

Jeremiah 21:8 "Now you shall say to this people, thus says the Lord: behold I set before you the way of life and the way of death."

Declare Today

I will tell others that Jesus is the way of life, eternal life!

Remember

Stay in the Spirit!

Day 7

What does Matthew 7:13-14 say to you? What is God saying to you? What was your takeaway from this week's topic? Notes.

WEEK 7

HONOR GOD IN YOUR GIVING

The Scripture

Proverbs 3:9-10 "Honor the Lord with your possessions and with the first fruits of all your increase so your Barns will be filled with plenty and your vats will overflow with new wine."

The Experience

I was taught to honor God with my giving although there is much controversy within the church when it comes to Gods principles on giving a tenth or any of our income to God's Kingdom. I sincerely say; ask God! Actively giving into the Kingdom of God was one of the best decisions I ever made. I can remember being in church during a tithing message, and the Holy Spirit suggested that I began to honor God in my giving, and I agreed. The moment I agreed within my heart, the promises in the scriptures became alive to me. I always knew giving was good; it was in my blood. (I got it from my mama). My message usually encourages others to study the word for a personal relationship with the Trinity, and to be a good steward over the people, talents, and finances which God has blessed us to have in our lives. I just believe that if we know God's word for our self, we can reap the benefits of it. God's word on the subject of tithing is not just beneficial financially, but it's also good for the soul; it builds trust, it's everlasting and most of all, it honors God. I would like to challenge you to allow God's word to penetrate your heart on the subject of giving and expect the promises of God to manifest in your life.

The Word

"For God so loved the world that he gave his only begotten Son that you and I might have life and have it more abundantly" John 3:16. Father God gave us His best when He gave us Jesus the ultimate sacrifice, we cannot beat God giving. God's word says that He will bless generation upon generation of those that honor Him. God has a lot to say about giving. In Malachi 3:10 He promises to rebuke the devour for our sake, and in Luke 6:38 He promises it will be given to us in the same measure in which we give.

Daily Prayer: Lord, father God, thank you for giving me the desire to want to give to your Kingdom, thank you for all that you have blessed me with. I thank you for this opportunity to serve you in giving of my tithes and offerings, my gifts and talents. In your Son Jesus name, I pray Amen!

DAILY SCRIPTURES FOR MEDITATING

Day 1

Lev 27:30-32 "All the tithe of the land whether of the seed of the land or of fruit of the tree is the Lords, it is holy to the Lord."

Declare today

All the Tithe is Holy and belongs to the Lord!

Remember

Tithing is Gods financial plan for His Kingdom.

Day 2

Malachi 3:10-11 "Bring all the tithes into the storehouse that there may be food in my house and try me now in this says the Lord of host if I will not open up for you the windows of heaven and pour out for you such a blessing that there will not be room enough to receive it. And I will rebuke the devourer for your sakes so that he will not destroy the fruit of your ground nor shall the vine fail to bear fruit for you in the field says the Lord of host."

Declare Today

I will try the Lord in my Giving.

Remember

Tithes and offerings are used for the daily functions of Gods Church.

Day 3

Matthew 6:24 "No one can serve two masters for either he will hate the one and love the other or else he will be loyal to the one and despise the other you cannot serve God and Mammon."

Declare Today

I will serve God with my giving!

Remember

Put God first!

Day 4

Matthew 6:21 "for where your treasure is, there your heart will be also."

Declare Today

I will purposely keep my heart in God's Kingdom.

Remember

Study God's word on the subject of tithing.

Day 5

Luke 6:38 "give and it will be given to you good measure pressed down shaken together and running over will be put into your bosom for with the same measure that you use it will be measured back to you."

Declare Today

I will give cheerfully.

Remember

Trust God for what to give, when to give, and who to give to.

Day 6

John 14:15 "If you love me keep my commandments."

Declare Today

I love God, and I will honor Him in my giving.

Remember

Honor God by loving others!

Day 7

Have your thoughts on giving changed? If yes, How? What is God saying to you? What was your takeaway from this week's topic? Notes.

WEEK 8

THE WORD IS LIFE!

The Scripture

Deuteronomy 8:3 "So he humbled you, allowed you to hunger, and fed you a manna which you did not know nor did your fathers know, that he might make you know that man shall not live by bread alone: but man lives by every word that proceeds from the mouth of the Lord."

The Experience

The word works, if you work it! This catchy phrase I picked up somewhere in my late teens, or early twenties, I quickly realized that it is true. When I graduated high school, I received a red cover, small print, KJV Bible and I loved it, I used the word to help me overcome obstacles like fear, guilt, and shame. There was nothing the word could not help me with, I was not always faithful to the word, but the word was always faithful to me.

The word of God transforms us from the inside out. To know the word is to know Jesus; He is the authority of God's word. Everything we need is in the word. The word is life! As I look back over my life, I can see how anytime I submitted my will over to Jesus, the word was able to penetrate my heart bringing about a change on the inside of me. The scriptures say we are to be imitators of Christ, the more we submit to the Lord the more like Him we become, Faith arises, and we begin to pray different, we talk different, and we walk different.

A life totally submitted to Christ will bear good fruit, humble yourself under the mighty hand of God and He shall lift you up!

The Word

John 1:14 "And the Word became flesh and dwelt among us, and we beheld his glory, the glory as the only begotten of the father, full of grace and truth." The scriptures tell us that the word is life, and that there is power in the word. Jeremiah says that he ate the word. Every word in the Bible is inspired by the Holy Spirit. We can live off o the Knowledge of the word, the wisdom in the word and the power produced by the word. The word is life! When we are living a life totally submitted to Christ (the word), then we can resist the devil causing him to flee **James 4:7**.

Daily Prayer: Lord-Father-God, thank you for your word, your grace and your mercy. Father, thank you for giving me a desire to know you, Jesus and the Holy Spirit through the word. Engraft your word on to me that I may know and experience its power, in Jesus name I Pray! Amen!

DAILY SCRIPTURES FOR MEDITATING

Day 1

John 1:1 "In the beginning was the Word and the Word was with God and the Word was God. He was in the beginning with God. All things were made through him and without him nothing was made that was made. In him was the life, and the life was the light of men"

Declare Today

Jesus is the word, the word is the life, and the life is the light.

Remember

The word is your life.

Day 2

John 1:14 "And the Word became flesh and dwelt among us, and we beheld his glory, the glory as the only begotten of the father, full of grace and truth."

Declare Today

Jesus is the word, truth and grace!

Remember

To know the word is to know Jesus.

Day 3

Hebrews 4:12 "For the word of God is living and powerful, and sharper than any two edge-sword piercing even to the division of soul and spirit, and of joints and marrow, and is a discerner of the thoughts and intents of the heart."

Declare Today

The word of God overflows with power.

Remember

The word is alive.

Day 4

James 1:21 "Therefore lay aside all filthiness and overflow of wickedness, and receive with meekness the implanted word, which is able to save your souls."

Declare Today

The Word is our savior.

Remember

The word is a gift, received it!

Day 5

"1 Colossians 3:16 Let the word of Christ dwell in you richly in all wisdom, teaching and admonishing one another in Psalms and hymns and spiritual songs, singing with grace in your hearts to the Lord."

Declare Today

The word will dwell in us richly if we let it.

Remember

The word is full of grace

Day 6

Titus 1:9 "Holding fast the faithful word as he has been taught, that he may be able, by sound doctrine, both to exhort and convict those who contradict."

Declare Today

I will hold fast to the faithful word, so that I may exhort or convict anyone or thing that contradicts it.

Remember

The word is truth.

Day 7

Can you dedicate time (more time) to study the word of God? What is God saying to you? What was your takeaway from this week's topic? Notes.

WEEK 9

TROUBLE IN MY WAY.

The Scripture

John 16:33 "These things have I spoken to you, that in me you may have peace. In the world you will have tribulation; but be of good cheer, I have overcome the world."

The Experience

While experiencing some rough days financially (experiencing a complete financial upset) after doing my best to walk with the Trinity to honor, respect, and reverence the Lord. I went to Jesus seeking an understanding of what I was experiencing, after all He promised me safety in His arms. Jesus showed me that seeds are buried, caterpillars are confined to a cocoon, olives are shaken, beaten and pressed, in the process of fulfilling a higher purpose! In the process of being disciplined in the things of God, we must experience some things. He explained to me that if I experience it, then I can testify about it because surely in Him I shall overcome, assuring me that big responsibilities mean bigger possibilities.

The Word

Jesus is saying take heart, for He has overcome the world. He invites us to have peace knowing that in this world, we may have tribulations, but through faith in Him, we shall overcome! We are just travellers in a foreign land, a fallen world. Christ is seated with the Father and faith in Him gives us access! Jesus knows what it means to be Crucified; He did it for us! **John 14: 6** tells us that Jesus is the way; Take heart!

Daily prayer: Lord father God, thank you! Thank you for giving me the comfort in knowing that even in the troubles of this world, I can find peace in you. Thank you father that my troubles were meant to make me stronger, and to equip me for a greater purpose for the kingdom! Thank you father, I love you and appreciate you in Jesus name I pray amen!

DAILY SCRIPTURE FOR MEDITATING

Day 1

1John 4:4 "You are of God little children, and have overcome them, because he who is in you is greater than he who is in the world."

Declare Today

The Christ in me is greater than He who is in the world!

Remember

Be expecting greater.

Day 2

1John 5:4 "For whatever is born of God overcomes the world and this is the victory that has overcome the world our faith."

Declare Today

Victory is in my Faith!

Remember

You are an overcomer.

Day 3

1 Samuel 26:24 "And indeed, as your life was valued much this day in my eyes, so let my life be valued much in the eyes of the Lord and let him deliver me out of all tribulation."

Declare Today

When I value the lives of others, God values my life and delivers me from all my troubles!

Remember

Look for the Godly value in every situation!

Day 4

1 Peter 1:6 "In this you greatly rejoice, though now for a little while, if need be, you have been grieved by various trials."

Declare Today

I will rejoice even in my trials.

Remember

Be of good cheer!

Day 5

Acts 14:22 "Strengthening the souls of the disciples exhorting them to continue in the faith, and saying, we must through many tribulations enter the kingdom of God."

Declare Today

Even through tribulation, I must continue in faith.

Remember

Be not afraid!

Day 6

James 1:2 "My brother count it all joy, when you fall into various trials."

Declare Today

I shall count it all joy.

Remember

Be joyful, laugh in the face of your trials.

Day 7

What does peace mean to you? What is God saying to you? What was your takeaway from this week's topic? Notes.

WEEK 10

A SUBMITTED LIFE.

The Scripture

James 1:22-24 "But be doers of the word and not hearers only deceiving yourselves. For if anyone is a hearer of the word and not a doer, he is like a man observing his natural face in a mirror, for he observes himself, goes away and immediately forgets what kind of man he was."

The Experience

Jesus says, why do you call me Lord, and don't do what I say; I learned that when I submit myself to Jesus as my Savior, I also had to accept Him as my Lord. Being submitted to Jesus as my Lord, I grew close enough to discern His voice. Thank God! He humbled me enough that obedience was my reaction. In this experience, I became not just a hearer of the word but a doer also.

The Word

James 1:22 "But be doers of the word and not hearers only deceiving yourselves. God's word tells us to hear and do! In every area of our lives, we are to hear the word and apply it! Hear wisdom and understanding. Hear and proclaim the word. Hear quickly and speak slowly. It is important for us to not only hear the word but do what we hear.

Daily Prayer: Lord Father God, I submit my life to you, you are welcome in every situation of my life, thank you for answering my prayers, when I seek you for wisdom and counsel, thank you for directing my steps, thank you for giving me a ear to hear your word and faith to do it, in Jesus name I pray!

Amen!

DAILY SCRIPTURE FOR MEDITATING

Day 1

Jeremiah 11:6 "Then the Lord said to me, proclaim all these words in the cities of Judah and in the streets of Jerusalem, saying hear the word of this Covenant and do them."

Declare Today

I will hear the word of the Lord and obey it!

Remember

Do not hear the word only, do the word also!

Day 2

Proverbs 12:15 "The way of a fool is right in his own eyes, but he who heeds counsel is wise."

Declare Today

I will pay attention to, listen to, and consider wise counsel.

Remember

Observe and obey the word.

Day 3

Proverbs 18:13 "He who answers a matter before he hears it, it is a folly and a shame to him."

Declare Today

I will practice hearing a matter out.

Remember

Search the scriptures and apply them to your life.

Day 4

Proverbs 19:27 "cease listening to instructions, my son, and you will stray from the words of knowledge."

Declare Today

I will not stray from words of knowledge.

Remember

Do not forget that Jesus is the Word.

Day 5

Proverbs 5:1 "My son, pay attention to my wisdom; lend your ear to my understanding."

Declare Today

I will listen to the wisdom and understanding of God and apply it to my life.

Remember

Loudly proclaim that the word is your life.

Day 6

Proverbs 11:14b "Where there is no counsel, the people fall; but in the multitude of counselors there is safety."

Declare Today

I will seek Godly counsel when I need it!

Remember

Gods counsel can be found in His Kingdom people!

Day 7

What is your favourite scripture? What word are you standing on? What is God saying to you? What was your takeaway from this week's topic? Notes.

WEEK 11

IT'S A MATTER OF HEART

⟨∞⟩

The Scripture

Deuteronomy 6:5 "You shall love the Lord your God with all your heart, with all your soul, and with all your strength."

The Experience

During my walk with the Lord, I have learned that it's a matter of the heart. On many occasions, I have experienced that as soon as I purposed in my heart to make a change in Gods direction, the Lord moved on my behalf and the results always ended with greater revelation and growth for me. God wants our hearts most of all!

The Word

Proverb 3:5 Trust in the Lord with all thy heart and lean not on your own understanding; In all thy ways acknowledge him and he shall direct your path. The Lord wants our whole heart, He wants us to willingly hide His word in our hearts and to love Him with all our strength, and He promises to show us favor.

Daily Prayer: Father God, Thank you Lord, for a renewed mind and a repentant heart. Thank you for placing a desire on the inside of us to seek you with our whole heart! Thank you, Lord, for all that you do on our behalf. Lord I humble myself before you, have your way in Jesus name I pray, Amen!

DAILY SCRIPTURES FOR MEDITATION:

Day 1

Psalm 51:17 "The sacrifices of God are a broken spirit, A broken and contrite heart—These, O God, you will not despise."

Declare Today

I will humble myself before the Lord.

Remember

God wants my heart.

Day 2

Deuteronomy 6:5 "And these words which I command you today shall be in your heart."

Declare Today

I will hide the word of God in my heart!

Remember

Your heart belongs to the Lord!

Day 3

Ezekiel 36:26 "I will give you a new heart and put a new spirit within you I would take the heart of stone out of your flesh and give you a heart of flesh."

Declare Today

I am willing to receive a new heart and new spirit from the Lord.

Remember

God will give you a new heart!

Day 4

Deuteronomy 6:5 "You shall love the Lord your God with all your heart, with all your soul, and with all your strength."

Declare Today

I love the Lord Jehovah God with my whole heart!

Remember

Love God unconditional!

Day 5

Psalm 84:2 "How my soul longs, yes, even faints for the courts of the Lord: My heart and my flesh cry out for the living God."

Declare Today

My soul and heart thirst for the living God!

Remember

God welcomes a repentant heart.

Day 6

Proverbs 3:3-4 "Let not mercy and truth forsake you: bind them around your neck, write them on the tablet of your heart, and so find favor and high esteem in the sight of God and man."

Declare Today

If I keep the word of the Lord close to my heart, I shall find favor in the sight of God and man!

Remember

Keep Gods word first in your situation!

Day 7

Do you trust God? What is God saying to you? What was your takeaway from this week's topic? Notes.

WEEK 12

HE SEEKS THE LOST.

The Scripture

Matthew 18:11-14 "For the son of man has come to save that which was lost. What do you think, if a man has a hundred sheep, and one of them goes astray, does he not leave the ninth-nine and go to the mountains to seek the one that is straying? "And if he should find it, assuredly, I say to you he rejoices more over that sheep then over the ninety-nine that did not go astray. "Even so it is not the will of the father who is in heaven that one of these little ones should perish."

The Experience

Oftentimes in life, we are lost and don't even recognize it! But God is faithful, and He does not leave us lost, He seeks us out and nurtures us until we are able to follow Him. God invites us to follow Him; it is His will and desire that we are not lost, so He guides us along the way. God speaks to us through Jesus, the Holy Spirit and oftentimes, the direction comes from other people. Sometimes, anointed men and women are chosen just to help you or me get on the path that the Lord has destined for us. We are never so lost that He can't find us! The Lord will leave the ninety-nine for the one (for you)!

The Word

Jesus says **John 6:37** "All that the Father gives Me will come to Me, and the one who comes to Me I will by no means cast out. It is the will of the Father that everyone be saved, God Himself will tug on the hearts of His people, He is patient with us and leads us to repentance. It is the desire of the Lord that all His children be delivered from places of destruction. Jesus seeks the lost and baptizes them with the Holy Spirit and Fire.

Daily Prayer: My Lord and Savior Jesus Christ, thank you for your passion to save me. Thank you for pursuing me and knocking on the door of my heart. Thank you father that I am the apple of your eye. In Your name Jesus I pray! Amen!

DAILY SCRIPTURE FOR MEDITATING

Day 1

Ezekiel 34:11 "For thus says the Lord God: "Indeed I myself will search for my sheep and seek them out."

Declare Today

The Lord Himself seeks His lost.

Remember

God is omnipotent

Day 2

Ezekiel 34:12 "As a shepherd seeketh out his flock on the day he is among his scattered sheep; so, will I seek out my sheep and deliver them from all the places where they were scattered on a cloudy and dark day."

Declare Today

The Lord will seek us even in our darkest days.

Remember

Jesus is my shepherd.

Day 3

Luke 19:10 "For the Son of Man has come to seek and to save that which was lost."

Declare Today

Jesus seeks and saves the lost.

Remember

Jesus loves you.

Day 4

Luke 3:16 "John answered, saying to all, I indeed baptize you with water; but one mightier than I is coming, who sandal strap I am not worthy to loose. He will baptize you with the Holy Spirit and fire."

Declare Today

Jesus comes with the Holy Spirit and fire.

Remember

Receive the baptism of the Holy Spirit.

Day 5

2 Peter 3:9 "The Lord is not slack concerning his promise, as some count slackness, but is long-suffering toward us, not willing that any should perish but that all should come to repentance."

Declare Today

The Lord is patient with us, and it is His desire that all come to repentance, all come to Him.

Remember

God is omnipresent.

Day 6

Deuteronomy 32:10 "He found him in a desert land and in the wasteland, a howling wilderness; He encircled him, He instructed him, He kept him as the apple of His eye."

Declare Today

I am the apple of God's eye, and He will find me no matter where I am.

Remember

Nothing can separate you from the love of God!

Day 7

Can you feel the Lord tugging at your heart? What is God saying to you? What was your takeaway from this week's topic? Notes.

WEEK 13

THE FOUNDATION FOR OUR RELATIONSHIP WITH THE TRINITY.

The Scripture

1 Corinthians 3:10-11 "According to the grace of God, which was given to me, as a wise master builder I have laid the foundation, and another builds on it. But let each one take heed how he Builds on it. For no other foundation can anyone lay than that which is laid, which is Jesus Christ."

The Experience

Anything that's going to stand must first begin with a solid foundation; it doesn't matter if it's a house, a car, or simply planting a garden. We must start with a solid foundation, the right foundation. I have learned that if I use the word of God as the foundation for making everyday decisions on a consistent basis, my life is more fruitful and I find myself demonstrating God's purpose for my life! The foundation of our life should be built on every word of God. The word is our life!

The Word

In Matthew chapters 5, 6, Jesus was preaching and teaching the disciples how to build a solid foundation. Jesus wants us to hear the same things He taught them; we are the salt of the earth, the light of the world. He says that we should love our enemies, bless those who curse us and pray for those who spitefully use and persecute us. He talked about anger, lust, divorce and taking oaths. Jesus taught on love, forgiveness, prayer, and fasting. He has given us the blueprint to building a solid relationship with the Trinity.

Daily Prayer: Our heavenly Holy father Jesus Christ, Lord, thank you! Thank you that you are my rock, my sure foundation. Lord, we rest and depend upon your every word. Thank you for your faithfulness, your grace and your mercy in your name Jesus I pray! Amen!

DAILY SCRIPTURE FOR MEDITATING

Day 1

Matthew 7:24 "Therefore whoever hears these sayings of mine, and does them, I would like him to a wise man who built his house on the rock:"

Declare Today

Doing the word of God makes me wise and strengthens my foundation.

Remember

The word is a sure foundation

Day 2

Matthew 7:25 "And the rain descended, the floods came, and the winds blew and beat on that house; and it did not fall, for it was founded on the rock."

Declare Today

Although the storms of life come and beat upon my relationship with Jesus, my foundation will not be shaken, Jesus is a sure foundation.

Remember

Stay in the word.

Day 3

Acts 6:7 "The word of God spread, and the number of disciples multiplied greatly in Jerusalem, and a great many of the priest were obedient to the faith."

Declare Today

My obedience to the faith, strengthens the foundation of my relationship with The Trinity.

Remember

Stay within the boundaries of your foundation.

Day 4

Ephesians 2:19-21 "Now therefore, you are no longer strangers and foreigners, but fellow citizens with the saints and members of the household of God. Having been built on the foundation of the apostles and the prophets, Jesus Christ himself being the chief cornerstone, In Whom the whole building, being fitted

together, grows into a holy temple in the Lord."

Declare Today

We are building on a solid foundation when we imitate Jesus, the Apostles, and Prophets.

Remember

Stay committed to the principles of God.

Day 5

Isaiah 28:16 "Therefore thus says the Lord God: "Behold, I lay in Zion a stone for a foundation, A tried stone, a precious cornerstone, a sure foundation; whoever believes would not act hastily."

Declare Today

Jesus is the precious cornerstone, the sure foundation of my life.

Remember

Keep your eyes on Jesus!

Day 6

Matthew 5:48 "Be Ye therefore perfect, even as your Father in heaven is perfect."

Declare Today

I will imitate the Trinity and practice the beatitudes and commands in Matthew chapter 5.

Remember

I will imitate the attributes of the Trinity.

Day 7

Is your relationship with the Trinity built on a solid foundation? What is God saying to you? What was your takeaway from this week's topic? /Notes.

About Author

The author, Catherine Sterling Is a mother, grandmother, sister, ordained minister and CEO who has a heart for God's girls, young and older women alike, Catherine's heart is to encourage women to develop a more intimate personal relationship with the Trinity. Inviting whom ever will hear his voice to be one of God's Girls. You can always find Catherine sharing the love of God (Fisher of Men) and making disciples along the way. After writing Trinity's Girl 90-day devotional, you can find Catherine hard at work on her next assignment from the Lord!

Look for more Trinity's Girl Inspirations, as the Lord leads Catherine on this passionate journey of encouraging his Girls to draw near to him.

For comments or more information email us at Trinitysgirl1@gmail.com or to share a copy of this devotional with someone else visit our website at www.trinitysgirl.com

www.ingramcontent.com/pod-product-compliance
Lightning Source LLC
Chambersburg PA
CBHW021209020426
42331CB00003B/277